ALLIGATOR

Dylanna Press

Copyright © 2025 by Dylanna Press
Author: Tyler Grady

All rights reserved. No part of this publication may be reproduced, stored in a retrieval system, or transmitted by any means, including electronic, mechanical, photocopying, or otherwise, without prior written permission of the publisher.

Although the publisher has taken all reasonable care in the preparation of this book, we make no warranty about the accuracy or completeness of its content and, to the maximum extent permitted, disclaim all liability arising from its use.

Trademarks: Dylanna Press is a registered trademark of Dylanna Publishing, Inc. and may not be used without written permission.

ISBN: 978-1647904326 (pb); 978-1-64790-448-7 (hc)
Publisher: Dylanna Publishing, Inc.
First Edition: 2025
Printed in the United States of America
10 9 8 7 6 5 4 3 2 1

For information about special discounts for bulk purchases, please contact:

Dylanna Publishing, Inc.
www.dylannapublishing.com

Contents

Meet the Alligator　7

What Do Alligators Look Like?　8

Where Do Alligators Live?　11

Super Survivors – Alligator Adaptations　12

What Do Alligators Eat?　15

Do Alligators Have a Social Life?　16

On the Move　19

A Day in the Life　20

Mating and Birth　23

Growing Up Alligator　24

Alligators and Their Ecosystem　27

Natural Predators　28

Challenges and Threats　31

Life Span and Population　32

Conclusion　35

Test Your Alligator Knowledge!　36

STEM Challenge: Think Like a Scientist!　37

Word Search　38

Glossary　39

Resources and References　40

Index　41

Fun Fact: Alligators have barely changed in 8 million years. Their ancestors survived the extinction that wiped out the dinosaurs!

Meet the Alligator

SPLASH! Something powerful moves through the murky water. Only a pair of eyes and a snout peek above the surface. Then—*SNAP!*—a fish disappears in a flash of jaws. You've just seen one of Earth's oldest predators in action: the American alligator!

Alligators are large reptiles that live in the wetlands of the southeastern United States. You'll find them in swamps, marshes, rivers, and lakes from North Carolina to Texas. Florida and Louisiana have the biggest alligator populations in the world.

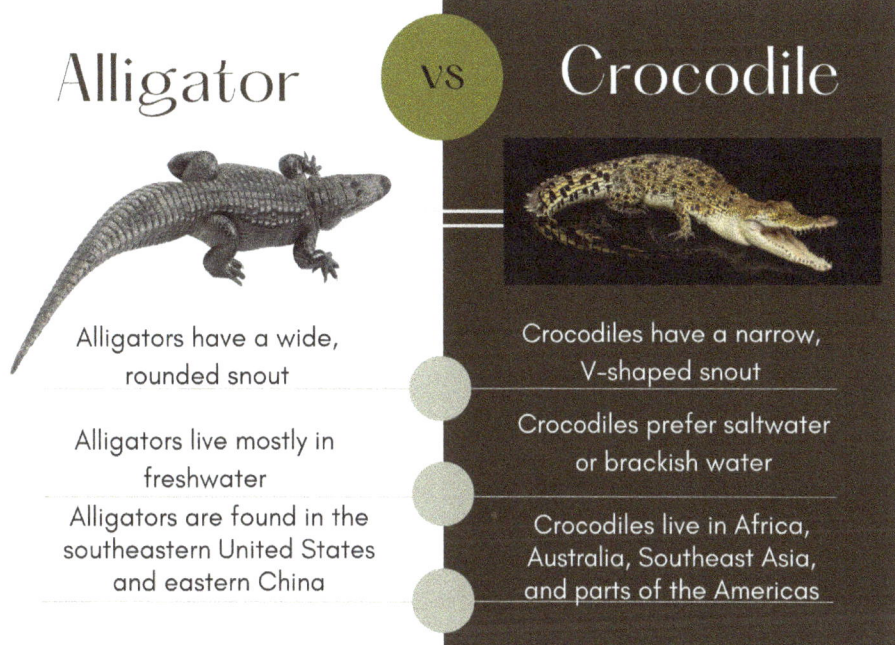

The American alligator (*Alligator mississippiensis*) is one of just two species of alligator—the other is the Chinese alligator, which lives near China's Yangtze River and is much smaller. Alligators belong to the Crocodylia order, which also includes crocodiles, caimans, and gharials.

These animals haven't changed much in millions of years. Their tough skin, powerful tails, and sharp teeth make them perfectly built for survival. Once endangered due to hunting and habitat loss, alligators are now a conservation success story—there are over 5 million of them alive today!

You might think of alligators as scary, but there's a lot more to these ancient animals than big teeth and loud bellows. Alligators are smart, strong, and important to their environment. By the time you finish reading, you might just think they're awesome, too.

What Do Alligators Look Like?

American alligators are some of the most impressive reptiles in the world. They have big, tough bodies designed for power and survival.

Adult males usually grow between 8 to 11 feet (2.4 to 3.4 meters) long, but some giants can reach up to 15 feet (4.6 meters)! Females are smaller, averaging around 6 to 9 feet (1.8 to 2.7 meters). A large male can weigh 400 to 800 pounds (180 to 360 kilograms), while females weigh 200 to 300 pounds (90 to 135 kilograms).

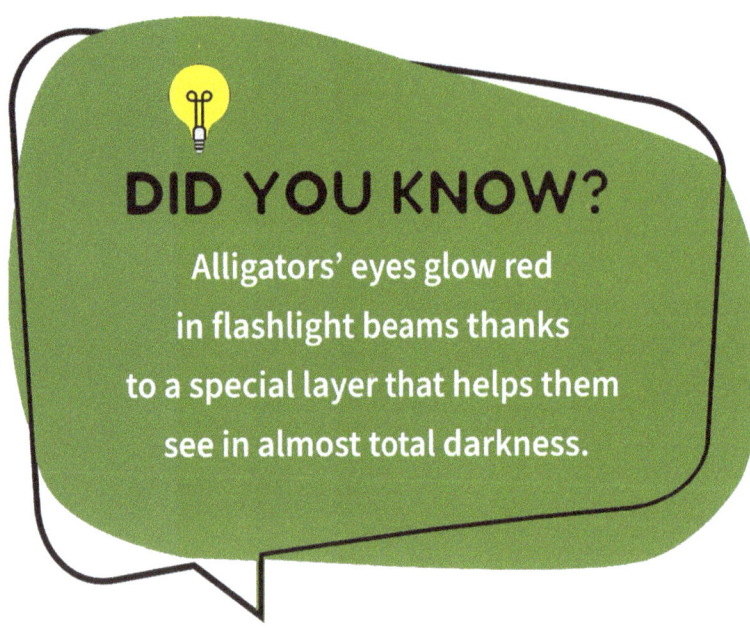

DID YOU KNOW?
Alligators' eyes glow red in flashlight beams thanks to a special layer that helps them see in almost total darkness.

An alligator's broad, U-shaped snout is one of its most recognizable features. It's strong enough to crush hard-shelled prey like turtles. Hidden just behind the snout are its eyes and nostrils, placed on top of its head so it can float almost entirely underwater while still seeing and breathing.

Covering the gator's body is a layer of tough skin packed with bony plates called osteoderms or scutes. These natural shields act like built-in armor, protecting the gator during fights or attacks.

Alligators have 74 to 80 sharp, cone-shaped teeth in their jaws at one time. These teeth grip and hold prey—they don't chew! As they break or wear down, new ones grow in, sometimes thousands over a lifetime. And when it bites down, an alligator can exert 2,000 p ounds per square inch (140 kg/cm²)—one of the strongest bites on Earth.

Their thick tail makes up about half their body length and helps them swim at speeds of up to 20 miles per hour (32 kilometers per hour). It's also a powerful weapon if the gator feels threatened.

They may look slow and clumsy, but don't be fooled—alligators are built for action.

Fun Fact: Young alligators have been spotted climbing trees to bask in the sun—some lounging on branches 6 feet off the ground!

Where Do Alligators Live?

American alligators are aquatic reptiles that thrive in the wetlands of the southeastern United States. Their native range stretches from North Carolina to eastern Texas, covering all the Gulf Coast states. These warm, swampy areas are perfect for a cold-blooded predator that loves water.

You'll find gators in freshwater swamps, marshes, rivers, lakes, and ponds—especially places with slow-moving water, thick vegetation, and lots of prey. Their streamlined bodies, powerful tails, and top-mounted eyes help them glide silently through these wetland worlds.

QUESTION
Do alligators ever leave the water?

ANSWER
Yes! They often bask on riverbanks or muddy shores to warm up in the sun. Sometimes they even travel short distances over land to find new water.

Alligators usually stick to freshwater, but they can survive in brackish water (a mix of salt and fresh) for short periods. In parts of Florida, you might even spot one in a mangrove swamp or coastal marsh! But unlike crocodiles, alligators can't stay in saltwater for long—they don't have the special salt glands that crocodiles use to survive in the sea.

The largest populations of American alligators live in Florida and Louisiana, where the warm climate and rainy seasons support huge wetland ecosystems. In fact, each state is home to over 1 million wild alligators!

Alligators also shape the land around them. They dig out "gator holes" that stay filled with water during dry months, providing homes for fish, birds, turtles, and more. These clever reptiles aren't just survivors—they're ecosystem engineers.

Even though they're cold-blooded, alligators have adapted to places with seasonal changes. In colder weather, they become less active and may burrow into dens to rest. It's not true hibernation, but it helps them stay safe and warm until the sun returns.

Super Survivors – Alligator Adaptations

Alligators are masters of survival. Every part of their body—from their skin to their lungs—has evolved to help them thrive in wetland habitats.

- **Built to Bite:** Alligators can slam their jaws shut with a force of up to 2,000 pounds per square inch (140 kg/cm²). But here's a surprise—the muscles that open their mouth are weak. That's why researchers can hold an alligator's mouth closed with just their hands or a strip of tape.

- **Stealth Hunters:** With their eyes, ears, and nostrils placed on top of their head, alligators can see, hear, and breathe while the rest of their body stays underwater. Their dark, scaly skin also helps them blend into the shadows of the swamp.

- **Armor and Protection:** Rows of bony plates called osteoderms lie beneath their skin, forming natural body armor. These protect alligators during fights and from predators when they're young.

- **Underwater Experts:** Alligators are equipped with large lungs and a slow, efficient heart rate that lets them stay underwater for up to two hours while resting. A clear third eyelid, called a nictitating membrane, acts like goggles—shielding their eyes while they hunt below the surface.

- **Temperature Control:** Being cold-blooded means they can't produce body heat. Alligators regulate their temperature by moving between sun and shade or switching between land and water. In freezing weather, they can even poke their nostrils above the ice and enter a state of dormancy until it warms up.

- **Tail Power:** The long, muscular tail isn't just for swimming—it's also used for defense and stores fat for times when food is hard to find.

- **A Taste for Salt:** Alligators prefer freshwater, but they can handle brackish water for short periods thanks to special salt-excreting glands—though not as well as crocodiles.

These adaptations make alligators incredibly successful predators and have helped them survive for millions of years in their wetland habitats.

Fun Fact: Alligators swallow rocks on purpose! These "gastroliths" help grind up food and add weight for easier diving.

What Do Alligators Eat?

Alligators are opportunistic carnivores, which means they'll eat almost anything they can catch—and their menu changes as they grow.

Hatchlings and young alligators feed on small prey like insects, snails, worms, frogs, and tiny fish. They need to eat often to fuel their fast-growing bodies.

As they get bigger, juveniles expand their diet to include larger fish, snakes, birds, turtles, and small mammals. Their stronger jaws and quicker reflexes help them tackle tougher prey.

DID YOU KNOW?

Some alligators balance sticks on their snouts to lure nest-building birds close enough to grab. Sneaky!

Adult alligators are apex predators. With a bite force strong enough to crush bone and shell, they've been known to eat deer, raccoons, wild pigs, water birds, and even other alligators. In coastal areas, they may also eat crabs, shrimp, and other crustaceans.

They don't need to eat often. A large adult might only have 15 to 20 big meals per year. During cold months, they may not eat at all—living off fat stored in their tails while their metabolism slows down.

Alligators are ambush hunters. They wait quietly in the water, with only their eyes and nostrils visible. When prey comes close, they lunge with explosive speed. They don't chew their food—they tear it into chunks, swallow it whole, or use the "death roll" to twist off pieces.

They also act as nature's cleanup crew, feeding on carrion (dead animals) when available. Their strong stomach acids can digest bones, shells, and tough tissue that many other animals can't.

Do Alligators Have a Social Life?

Alligators may seem like silent loners, but they actually have a surprisingly complex social structure—especially for reptiles.

Most adult alligators are solitary hunters, each patrolling their own territory. But during certain times of year or when conditions force them closer together, they gather in groups called congregations. These gatherings happen most often during mating season or in droughts, when shrinking water sources bring many gators into the same area.

Even without permanent groups, alligators have a clear dominance hierarchy. Larger, older alligators often get the best spots, like sunny banks or deeper pools. Instead of constant fighting, they use body language to show their status. A dominant gator might raise its head and upper body high in the water—a clear sign to others to back off. While physical confrontations can happen, especially between males during mating season, serious injuries are rare.

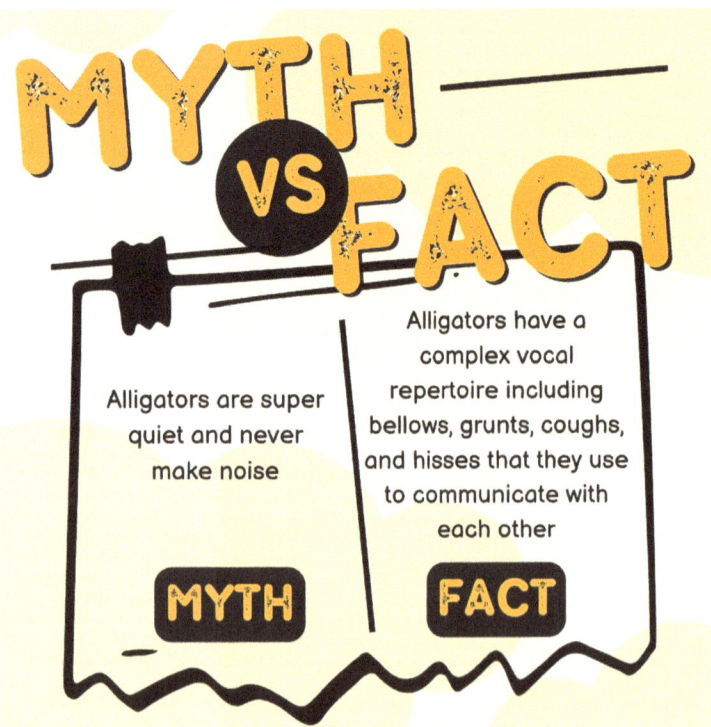

Alligators also communicate through sound and body movements. During the breeding season, males produce deep, rumbling bellows that can be heard from far away. These sounds serve a dual purpose: attracting females and warning rival males. Head-slaps, tail-swishes, and even bubble-blowing are all ways alligators send messages.

Young alligators are more social than adults. After hatching, they often stick together in groups called pods, which help protect them from predators like birds, raccoons, and even larger alligators. In some cases, juveniles remain close to their mother for up to three years—a rare trait among reptiles and a big boost to their survival.

Fun Fact: Male alligators bellow so powerfully during mating season that water on their backs "dances" and sprays into the air!

DID YOU KNOW?

Alligators can slow their heartbeat to just 2-3 beats per minute, helping them stay underwater for up to two hours!

On the Move

Alligators may look lazy while basking in the sun, but they can be surprisingly active and mobile creatures. Adult alligators establish and maintain **territories** that vary greatly in size depending on habitat quality, food availability, and the alligator's size.

A male alligator's territory typically ranges from a few acres up to 2,000 acres (8 square kilometers) of wetland habitat. Females usually maintain smaller territories, especially when they're caring for young. Within these territories, alligators create and use regular trails both in water and on land, sometimes worn into clear paths from years of use.

While not truly **migratory**, alligators do make seasonal movements within their home ranges. During mating season in spring, males may travel considerable distances searching for females. In winter, when temperatures drop, alligators move to deeper water that stays warmer or dig out "gator holes"—den-like depressions that fill with water and provide shelter from the cold.

Alligators mark their territories using scent glands located under their jaws. By rubbing their chin on logs or vegetation, they leave behind a musky odor that signals their presence to other alligators. Males also announce their territory through loud bellowing calls and by creating "water dances"— vibrating their bodies to make water droplets bounce above the surface.

Though they spend much of their time in water, alligators can travel surprising distances over land. During dry periods or when searching for new habitat, they've been documented traveling up to 10 miles (16 km) across land. These overland journeys typically happen at night when their dark skin provides better camouflage and the cooler temperatures prevent them from overheating.

A Day in the Life

Alligators follow a predictable rhythm most of the year, carefully balancing energy, temperature, and survival. Their activity depends on the season, the temperature, and even the time of day.

They are most active at dawn and dusk. These cooler parts of the day are perfect for hunting and patrolling their territory. During the warmer months, early mornings usually start with basking. Alligators relax on sunny banks, logs, or patches of floating vegetation to soak up heat. As cold-blooded reptiles, they need the sun's warmth to raise their body temperature and get moving.

Once they're warmed up, they become more alert. Some patrol their territory using well-worn trails, while others float quietly with only their eyes and nostrils exposed, waiting for prey. Hunting usually happens during the cooler parts of the day or at night, when alligators have the advantage with their excellent night vision and ability to sense ripples in the water.

DID YOU KNOW?

Alligators use the position of the sun to navigate back to familiar territories.

During the hottest part of the day, especially in summer, alligators retreat into the water to avoid overheating. They may float near the surface or rest at the bottom of deeper pools. When resting, they can stay submerged for up to two hours at a time.

Unlike mammals, alligators don't experience deep sleep. Instead, they enter resting periods where they close their eyes but remain partially alert. Part of their brain stays active, allowing them to react quickly if danger—or an easy meal—appears. They can rest both in water and on land, though they're more vulnerable during basking. As evening falls and temperatures cool, alligators often become active again, resuming hunting and territorial patrols.

In winter, alligators become sluggish, spending long periods in deeper, warmer water. They may go weeks without eating, relying on stored body fat to survive until spring returns.

Fun Fact: Gator holes become life-saving water sources during droughts—fish, turtles, birds, and deer all depend on them to survive.

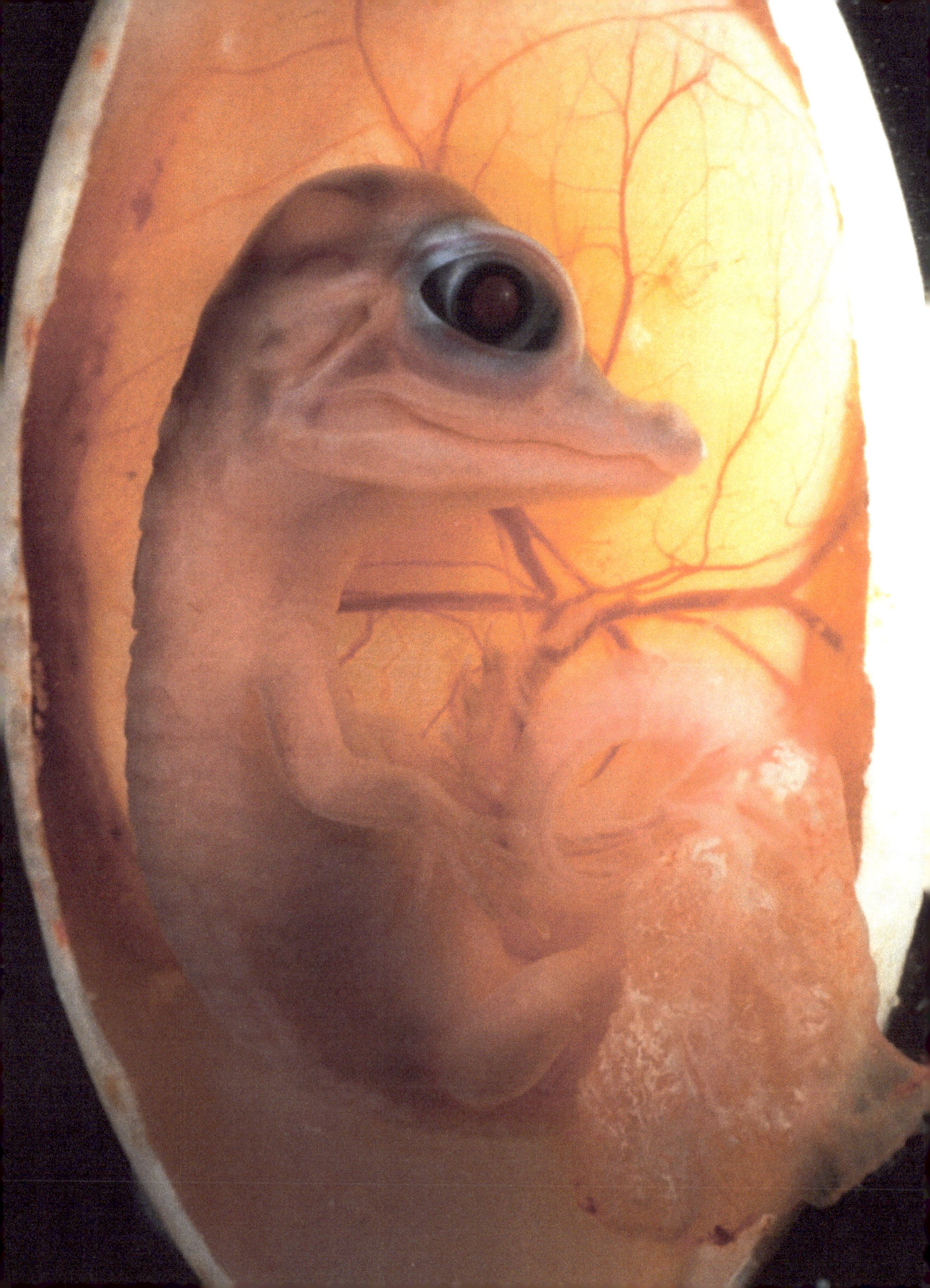

Mating and Birth

Springtime in the swamp brings more than just buzzing insects and blooming flowers—it also kicks off alligator mating season which typically begins in spring when water temperatures warm to above 70°F (21°C). Males start the process with impressive courtship displays. They produce deep, rumbling bellowing sounds while vibrating their bodies underwater, making the surface ripple and sending water droplets dancing into the air. These "water dances" show off their strength and size to both females and rival males.

Males compete for the attention of females, sometimes engaging in pushing contests or fights. The larger, more dominant males usually win these competitions and earn the right to mate with multiple females.

After mating, the males and females part ways. The males continue searching for more mates, while the females prepare for the next critical stage: nest building.

In June or July, a female builds a nest near the water's edge. She piles up mud, grasses, and other plants into a mound about 3 to 5 feet wide (1 to 1.5 meters) and 2 to 3 feet high (0.6 to 0.9 meters). This nest not only protects the eggs from predators but also uses heat from the rotting vegetation to help incubate them.

INSIDE AN ALLIGATOR NEST

Vegetation layer: Decomposing plants create heat for incubation

Mother guards the nest day and night

20-50 leathery eggs buried in the center of the nest

Mud and soil help keep the nest strong and moist

Temperature inside nest decides if babies are male or female!

The female lays between 20 and 50 eggs, carefully covering them with more vegetation. Here's something amazing: the temperature inside the nest decides whether the babies will be male or female!

- Eggs kept below 86°F (30°C) become females
- Eggs kept above 93°F (34°C) become males

The mother alligator stays close to the nest throughout the 65-day incubation period, protecting it from predators like raccoons and birds. When the eggs are ready to hatch, the babies make high-pitched calls from inside their eggs. These sounds alert the mother, who carefully uncovers the nest and sometimes even helps crack open eggs by gently rolling them in her mouth.

Growing Up Alligator

Baby alligators, called hatchlings, enter the world at just 6–8 inches (15–20 centimeters) long and weighing only 2 ounces (57 grams). Despite their small size, they are miniature versions of adult alligators, complete with strong jaws, sharp teeth, and quick reflexes—just much more vulnerable.

As soon as they hatch, young alligators begin yelping with high-pitched calls. These sounds alert their mother, who carefully digs them out of the nest and carries them in her mouth to the water. This gentle transportation is remarkable considering the crushing power of an adult alligator's jaws.

After reaching the water, hatchlings often stay together in groups called pods. Staying in a pod offers protection from predators like birds, raccoons, fish, and even larger alligators. The mother remains nearby, guarding her young and responding quickly to distress calls. Her fierce protection is crucial—less than 10–15% of hatchlings survive to adulthood in the wild.

Growing Up Timeline

HATCHLING
2 ounces (57 grams)
Break out of their eggs using a special "egg tooth"

0-6 MONTHS
Grow to 1–2 feet (30–60 cm) long; stay close to mom for protection
Eat insects, small fish, and frogs

6-12 MONTHS
Double or triple in size
Begin catching larger prey

1-2 YEARS
Grow about 1 foot (30 cm) per year; Begin leaving their mother's immediate area but stay near familiar waters

2-4 YEARS
Become more independent and territorial; compete for their own hunting spots and basking areas

Young alligators grow quickly, often gaining up to 12 inches (30 centimeters) per year during their early years. They start out eating insects, small fish, and frogs, expanding their diet as they grow larger.

Learning to hunt and survive starts almost immediately. Hatchlings practice snapping at insects, small fish, or even floating leaves. These playful behaviors help develop the coordination and reflexes they'll need as adult hunters.

Unlike many reptiles, young alligators are not completely independent at birth. They learn survival skills from their mother and each other, including how to find food, avoid danger, and navigate their watery world. This long learning period and maternal care are unusual among reptiles—and are key reasons why alligators have thrived for millions of years.

Fun Fact: Baby alligators hatch with a tiny "egg tooth" to break out of their shell. It falls off shortly after—they won't need it again!

Fun Fact: An alligator's bite is 2,000 pounds strong—but the muscles that OPEN their jaws are so weak you could hold their mouth shut with your hands!

Alligators and Their Ecosystem

Alligators aren't just powerful predators—they're vital to keeping wetlands alive and healthy. From digging water holes to balancing animal populations, alligators help their environment in many important ways.

- **Keystone Species:** Alligators have a much bigger impact on wetlands than their numbers alone suggest. They are called a keystone species because many other plants and animals rely on the spaces and balance they help create.

- **Alligator Holes:** When dry seasons hit, gators dig deep depressions called "gator holes." These hold water when ponds and rivers shrink, creating life-saving habitats for fish, turtles, birds, and amphibians. Gator holes often become biodiversity hotspots.

- **Nest Mounds:** Female alligators build huge mounds of plants and mud to lay their eggs. After the babies hatch, these raised nests are often taken over by turtles, snakes, birds, and even wetland plants looking for a dry place to grow.

- **Population Control:** Alligators keep wetlands balanced by hunting a wide range of prey: fish, frogs, turtles, snakes, and small mammals. By keeping prey populations in check, they prevent overpopulation that could damage the ecosystem.

- **Nutrient Cycling:** As alligators shed old skin and leave behind waste, they fertilize wetland plants and algae—the base of the food chain. Their leftover prey remains also feed scavengers like turtles, birds, and small carnivores, making sure nothing goes to waste.

- **Habitat Creation:** By moving through marshes and ponds, alligators create trails that let other animals travel and help water flow more freely through dense vegetation. This keeps wetlands healthier and more diverse.

- **Nature's Thermometer:** Scientists monitor alligator populations to check the health of wetlands. Thriving alligators mean a thriving ecosystem, full of clean water, balanced animal life, and rich plant growth

Protecting wetlands doesn't just protect alligators. Wetlands filter water, store rainfall, reduce flooding, and support thousands of species—including humans who depend on clean water and flood protection.

Natural Predators

In their swampy world, adult alligators have almost no natural enemies. Thanks to their powerful jaws, massive size, and thick armored skin, a fully-grown alligator sits at the very top of the food chain. Few creatures in the wetlands are brave—or foolish—enough to challenge them.

But that doesn't mean alligators are completely safe. Young alligators, and especially hatchlings, face danger at every turn. Raccoons, otters, herons, egrets, large fish, and even bigger alligators all see baby gators as easy prey. In fact, during their first year of life, only about one in five hatchlings survive. For a young alligator, staying hidden, staying close to the mother, and growing quickly are the best chances for survival.

DID YOU KNOW?

Alligators can survive frozen in ice with just their noses sticking out.

Even adult alligators have rare but serious threats. In Florida's Everglades, invasive Burmese pythons—giant snakes that don't belong in the environment—have been documented attacking and swallowing adult alligators. In parts of southern Florida, where American crocodiles and alligators share territory, a large crocodile might sometimes prey on a smaller adult alligator.

The greatest risk comes even earlier—in the nest. Alligator eggs are a favorite meal for predators like raccoons, opossums, bears, and birds. Mother alligators guard their nests fiercely. They stay nearby day and night throughout the two-month incubation period, hissing, lunging, and snapping at anything that comes too close.

When threatened, an alligator doesn't just rely on size. First, they use intimidation—hissing loudly, opening their mouths wide to show their teeth, and whipping their muscular tails across the water. If warning displays don't work, an alligator won't hesitate to bite or lash out with its powerful tail. Their tough, bony armor protects them against most bites and scratches—making them one of the best-defended animals in the wetlands.

Challenges and Threats

Aside from natural predators, alligators face other threats and challenges, many of which are human related. The biggest threat is **habitat loss**. Wetlands are drained for farms, roads, and buildings. As swamps and marshes disappear, alligators lose the places they need to live, hunt, and raise their young. Pollution adds to the problem. Chemicals, fertilizers, and waste can poison wetlands, making alligators sick, harming their food sources, and weakening their ability to reproduce.

Climate change is creating new risks too. Hotter temperatures, stronger storms, and longer droughts can dry up wetlands or destroy nests. Even more surprising, climate change can affect whether hatchlings are male or female, because the temperature of the nest decides the sex of baby alligators.

Collisions with humans are another growing danger. Roads that cut through wetlands create deadly crossings. Every year, especially during mating season when males travel farther, many alligators are hit by cars or injured by boats. Feeding by humans makes things worse. When people feed wild alligators, the animals lose their natural fear of humans. This can lead to dangerous encounters—and often results in the alligator being removed or killed for public safety.

Invasive species like the Burmese python also create problems. In places like the Everglades, these giant snakes compete with alligators for food and space—and sometimes even attack young gators. Illegal hunting and collection still happen too. Although legal hunting is carefully managed today, poachers sometimes kill alligators for their meat and skin. Young alligators are also sometimes illegally taken from the wild to be sold as exotic pets, a practice that rarely ends well for the animal.

How You Can Help Alligators

- **Protect Wetlands:** Support parks and wildlife refuges that protect swamps, rivers, and marshes.
- **Keep Wild Alligators Wild:** Never feed alligators. Feeding them makes them lose their natural fear of humans and can put both people and gators in danger.
- **Respect Wildlife Signs:** Stay alert near wetlands. Obey posted signs about alligator habitat and keep a safe distance if you see one.
- **Reduce Pollution:** Always throw away trash properly. Polluted water hurts alligators and many other wetland animals.
- **Learn and Share:** Teach others about how important alligators are to their ecosystems. The more people know, the more they care!

Life Span and Population

In the wild, most American alligators live between 35 and 50 years, although tracking their exact lifespan can be difficult. In captivity, with consistent food and veterinary care, they can live even longer, with some individuals reaching 60 to 70 years of age—the oldest recorded alligator lived to be over 80 years!

Alligators are one of America's greatest conservation success stories. In the 1950s, they were hunted nearly to extinction for their valuable hides. By 1967, the American alligator was listed as an endangered species throughout its range. Thanks to strict protection laws and conservation efforts, alligator populations recovered dramatically.

> **DID YOU KNOW?**
>
> Alligators never stop growing their entire lives! The oldest wild gators may be 50-70 years old.

Today, an estimated 5 million alligators live across the southeastern United States, with the largest numbers found in Florida (about 1.3 million) and Louisiana (about 2 million). Conservationists and wildlife managers work hard to monitor populations and protect wetlands, ensuring these ancient reptiles continue to thrive.

The alligator's protected status was changed from "endangered" to "threatened" in 1977, and in 1987, the U.S. Fish and Wildlife Service announced the American alligator had fully recovered throughout its range.

The current alligator population is considered stable and healthy in most areas. In some regions, populations have grown so successfully that carefully regulated hunting seasons have been established to manage numbers. These hunts help prevent overpopulation while providing economic benefits through the sustainable use of alligator meat and leather.

Conclusion

Throughout this book, we've explored what makes alligators such extraordinary and unique reptiles. From their prehistoric origins to their vital role in wetland ecosystems, alligators show us how wildlife and the natural world are deeply interconnected.

Alligators are full of surprises. Though they may seem slow-moving on land, they are powerful apex predators, perfectly built for survival in swamps, marshes, and rivers. They can hold their breath for long periods, regulate their body temperature using the sun and water, and communicate through deep bellows, hisses, and infrasound. Their armor-like scales, powerful tails, and crushing bite force have fascinated people for centuries.

These remarkable reptiles also teach an important lesson about balance. Alligators help maintain healthy wetlands by controlling prey populations and creating gator holes—lifesaving water sources for countless other species. By protecting alligators and their habitats, we help protect entire ecosystems and the many plants and animals that depend on them.

Today, alligators thrive in protected reserves and wild wetlands, a living example of how conservation and scientific research can work together to bring a species back from the brink. While threats like habitat destruction, pollution, and human conflict remain, ongoing conservation efforts give hope for their continued survival.

As we look to the future, alligators remind us that protecting biodiversity and fragile ecosystems is more important than ever. Through their resilience, ecological power, and ancient legacy, alligators show us that the wild is full of wonders—waiting to be protected and appreciated for generations to come.

Test Your Alligator Knowledge!

Ready to prove you know your gators? See how many questions you can answer!

1. How many species of alligator exist in the world?
    A) One B) Two C) Four D) Seven

2. What is the name for the bony plates under an alligator's skin that act like armor?
    A) Scales B) Osteoderms C) Gastroliths D) Keratin

3. About how many wild alligators live in the United States today?
    A) 500,000 B) 1 million C) 5 million D) 10 million

4. What determines whether a baby alligator will be male or female?
    A) Genetics from the parents B) The size of the egg C) The temperature of the nest D) What the mother eats

5. How long can an alligator hold its breath underwater while resting?
    A) 10 minutes B) 30 minutes C) Up to 2 hours D) Up to 5 hours

6. What are "gator holes" and why are they important?
    A) Burrows where alligators sleep at night B) Pools dug by alligators that provide water for other animals during droughts C) Nests where alligators lay their eggs D) Traps alligators dig to catch prey

7. What is an alligator's bite force?
    A) 500 pounds per square inch B) 1,000 pounds per square inch C) 2,000 pounds per square inch D) 5,000 pounds per square inch

8. Which U.S. state has the largest alligator population?
    A) Texas B) Florida C) Louisiana D) Georgia

9. What happens when people feed wild alligators?
    A) The alligators become healthier B) The alligators lose their fear of humans C) The alligators stop hunting other animals D) Nothing—it doesn't affect them

10. In what year was the American alligator declared fully recovered from endangered status?
    A) 1967 B) 1977 C) 1987 D) 1997

Answer Key: 1-B, 2-B, 3-C, 4-C, 5-C, 6-B, 7-C, 8-C, 9-B, 10-C

STEM Challenge: Think Like a Scientist!

Alligators have thrived in wetlands for millions of years. Try these fun, hands-on science experiments to discover the secrets behind their survival!

Bite Force Experiment

Topic: Physics & Engineering

You'll Need:
Clothespin, rubber bands, small objects (marshmallows, grapes, crackers)

What to Do:

1. Squeeze the clothespin with your fingers—that's your "bite"
2. Now wrap rubber bands around the clothespin handles and squeeze again
3. Test how easily you can crush different objects with and without the rubber bands

What You'll Learn:
The rubber bands add resistance, making it harder to open the clothespin but giving you more crushing power—just like an alligator's jaw muscles! Alligators have incredibly strong closing muscles but weak opening muscles. That's why a person can hold a gator's mouth shut with their hands!

Floating Predator Challenge

Topic: Physics & Buoyancy

You'll Need:
Bathtub or large container, various objects (cork, apple, plastic toy, rock), modeling clay

What to Do:

1. Test which objects float with most of their body underwater and just a small part above the surface

2. Now try shaping modeling clay different ways—flat, round, hollow—to see which shape floats with just a tiny bit showing

3. Can you make something float like an alligator, with only "eyes and nostrils" above water?

What You'll Learn:
Alligators float with just their eyes and snout above the surface thanks to their body shape and lung capacity. By controlling how much air is in their lungs, they can sink or rise in the water—perfect for sneaking up on prey!

Word Search

```
S K U N O I T A L U P O P E G
T O E U H I M A F H C N P R N
N C W C Y W W V J L O Z O Y I
M A B V O W E S C I L T F R L
N R Y E L S O T T Q A E U A H
D N S W L U Y A L D M R I T C
P I W O P L T S E A H O L I T
R V A A M P O R T S N V C L A
O O M B A G P W U E Q D P O H
B R P D W C Y B S S M W S S K
I E A J W Z M U K W N W L I B
T S T T R A Y X T A T I B A H
E G U C L T E R R I T O R Y R
F G O A R M O R Z G I S M I I
O E N T Y I C Y S N E D I M C
R J S E L O O I Y S T S E N V
C S R U T Q A L L I G A T O R
E P Q B N E L I T P E R S M E
```

Adaptation	Ecosystem	Prey
Alligator	Eggs	Reptile
Ambush	Habitat	Snout
Armor	Hatchling	Solitary
Bellows	Nest	Swamp
Bite Force	Population	Territory
Carnivore	Predator	Wetlands

Glossary

adaptations – special body parts or behaviors that help animals survive in their environment

apex predator – an animal at the top of the food chain with no natural predators

biodiversity – the variety of different plants, animals, and other living things in an area

brackish water – water that is a mix of freshwater and saltwater

cold-blooded – an animal that cannot produce its own body heat and relies on the environment to regulate its temperature

conservation – protecting animals, plants, and natural places for the future

Crocodylia – the scientific order that includes alligators, crocodiles, caimans, and gharials

dormancy – a sleep-like state where an animal's body slows down to save energy

ecosystem – all the living things in an area and how they interact with each other and their environment

endangered species – a type of animal or plant at serious risk of dying out completely

hatchling – a baby animal that has just come out of its egg

incubation – keeping eggs warm so they can develop and hatch

infrasound – sounds so low that humans cannot hear them

invasive species – animals or plants that don't belong in an area and cause harm to native wildlife

juvenile – a young animal that is no longer a baby but not yet fully grown
nictitating membrane – a clear third eyelid that protects an animal's eye underwater

opportunistic carnivore – a meat-eater that will hunt and eat whatever prey is available

osteoderms – bony plates beneath the skin that act as natural armor (also called scutes)

reptile – a cold-blooded animal with scaly skin that lays eggs, such as alligators, snakes, and turtles

wetlands – areas where water covers the soil, like swamps, marshes, and bogs

Resources and References

Want to learn more about alligators and wetland wildlife? Check out these trusted books, websites, and organizations dedicated to understanding and protecting these ancient reptiles.

Books

The American Alligator by Steve Potts (Capstone Press) — Great photos and easy-to-read facts perfect for young alligator fans.

Alligators and Crocodiles by Gail Gibbons (Holiday House) — A beautifully illustrated introduction to these amazing reptiles and what makes them different.

National Geographic Readers: Alligators and Crocodiles by Laura Marsh — Packed with incredible photos and fun facts at just the right reading level.

Websites

National Geographic Kids – Alligator Facts
kids.nationalgeographic.com/animals/reptiles/facts/american-alligator
Fun facts, videos, and photos perfect for young readers learning about alligators.

San Diego Zoo Wildlife Alliance – American Alligator
animals.sandiegozoo.org/animals/american-alligator
Detailed information about alligator biology, behavior, and conservation.

Smithsonian's National Zoo – American Alligator
nationalzoo.si.edu/animals/american-alligator
Learn about alligators living at the zoo and in the wild.

National Wildlife Federation – American Alligator
nwf.org/Educational-Resources/Wildlife-Guide/Reptiles/American-Alligator
Explore alligator facts and discover how you can help protect wetland habitats.

For Young Scientists

Florida Fish and Wildlife Conservation Commission
myfwc.com/wildlifehabitats/profiles/reptiles/american-alligator
Official information on Florida's alligator population and living safely with gators.

U.S. Fish and Wildlife Service – American Alligator
fws.gov/species/american-alligator-alligator-mississippiensis
Learn how scientists helped bring alligators back from endangered status.

Keep Exploring!

If you enjoyed learning about alligators, explore other titles in the This Incredible Planet series to discover more amazing animals—from sea turtles to penguins to elephants—and the habitats they call home.

Index

A
adaptations, 12
appearance, 8

B
basking, 20
birth, 23
body language, 16
body temperature, 12, 20
Burmese pythons, 28, 31

C
carnivores, 15
carrion, 15
Chinese alligator, 7
climate change, 31
collisions, 31
communication, 16, 19, 23, 24
congregations, 16
conservation, 7, 32
courtship, 23
crocodiles, 7, 11

D
daily life, 20
diet, 15, 24

E
ecosystem, 27
eggs, 23
environment, 7, 11, 27
Everglades, 28, 31
eyes, 8, 12

F
females, 18, 23, 24
Florida, 7, 11, 28, 32

G
gator holes, 11, 19, 21, 27

H
habitat, 7, 11, 18, 27, 31
hatchlings, 24, 28
heartbeat, 18
hunting, 12, 15, 16, 20, 24, 28, 31

I
incubation period, 23, 28
invasive species, 28, 31

J
jaws, 8, 12, 26
juvenile alligators, 16, 24, 28

K
keystone species, 27

L
life span, 32
Louisiana, 7, 11, 32
lungs, 12

M
males, 16, 17, 18, 23
mating, 23
migration, 19

N
nests, 23, 27, 28
nostrils, 8, 12
nutrient cycling, 27

O
osteoderms, 8, 12

P
physical characteristics, 8, 12
pods, 16, 24
pollution, 31
population, 32
predators, 15, 24, 28
prey, 15, 27

R
reptiles, 7

S
scent glands, 19
scutes, 8
seasons, 11, 20
size, 8
sleep, 20
snout, 8
social structure, 16
speed, 8

T
tails, 12, 28
teeth, 8
territories, 19
threats, 28, 31

W
water dances, 19, 23
weight, 8
wetlands, 11, 27, 31

www.ingramcontent.com/pod-product-compliance
Lightning Source LLC
Chambersburg PA
CBHW040223040426
42333CB00051B/3432